# Believe in Better for Your Future

Your Guide to Holistic Retirement and Financial Planning

# Believe in Better for Your Future

## Your Guide to Holistic Retirement and Financial Planning

Michael K. Macke, CFP®

**YouSpeakIt**
P U B L I S H I N G
*The Easy Way
to Get Your Book
Done Right*™

www.YouSpeakItPublishing.com

ISBN: 978-1-945446-32-0

*For my family, who has always been there to teach me right and wrong and has supported me unconditionally.*

# *Acknowledgments*

Thank you to all my mentors throughout my journey in the financial planning world. You have ranged from managers, co-workers, clients, and business partners to family. A special thank you to Jeannette who has pushed and prayed for this first book to be written.

Finally, I could not have done any of this without Mom, Dad, Mim, Pip, Grandma, and Faf. The wisdom you have shared will be passed on as long as I'm around.

# Contents

# Introduction

This book is about real world things, the things that affect every one of us, that we need to take into consideration when working with someone to plan our future. This book is about understanding everything one must consider when creating a retirement plan. My book is about retirement and financial planning in a holistic manner.

This book is not about investments, stock markets, or annuities, but a completely different take on *finance*. Within these pages, you will find guidance for selecting a professional to work with. I also provide clarity around why your situation is going to be different from your neighbor's situation.

I am tired of Wall Street running the show. I am tired of people being sold without really understanding what they are purchasing. I am tired of financial advisors who talk over their clients' heads, who sell complex products that people don't understand.

I wrote this book because as soft spoken, gentle, and kind as I am, I feel like I am fighting a battle. I feel like I am at war with the standard practice of the financial services industry. In my opinion, the act of *service* seems to be missing from the financial services industry.

So, I am writing this as an instruction manual. Hopefully it works and you will get a lot out of it and learn from it.

Why should you read it?

Because your situation is unique and you need the best advice suited to your specific needs.

*Believe in Better for Your Future* is about understanding that you need to discern what is important in your life—what you care about—and making sure that all the available resources are working toward achieving your goals.

Wall Street and the financial world have always put profits above anything or anyone else. They use giant marketing companies and sales processes to sell you things that you don't need, don't understand, or shouldn't have. These sales tactics are not done with your best interests at heart.

That is why I left that world. I studied to become a certified financial planner because I wanted to help people plan for their future. My grandmother, who was financially well-off, experienced regrets in later years simply because she did not have anyone to advise her regarding her finances.

I teach people a way to eliminate that type of regret. After seeing how it affected my grandmother and hearing her stories about it, I knew that this was about more than investments. It is more than 401(k)s, mutual funds, stocks, and bonds. It's about what that money needs to do for you.

I am sharing this information with you to show you that there is a way to approach financial planning that will allow you to sleep at night, that will allow you to enjoy the fruits of your labor, your family, your loved ones, and your friends.

Please read with an open mind. This book will not tell you how to put together the best portfolio, or how to save for retirement. It will not tell you how to take your money out of your retirement accounts, or how to draft your legal documents. However, this book does talk about whom you need to work with and how to work with them to ensure that all those things are addressed.

There are professionals who can help you. In the pages of this book, I'm going to cover why it is important to do things the right way and why it's important to find someone who understands your long-term plans and goals. This guide will help you understand the bigger picture.

This book is different from other financial books because a lot of it comes from my heart, from what I have seen, and what I have done. I want you to read this and realize that there are good people out there that will help you the right way, and that will do what is in your best interest.

What I share in these pages will help you understand if your financial planner is considering all options. Additionally, you will know whether the person you are working with is doing things the right way or if they need to take a second look, or perhaps when a second opinion is needed for suggestions on what they could be doing differently.

I hope my message is passed along from grandparents to children and grandchildren, and to anyone that would benefit. I hope what I share here will have you asking yourself if you have considered all the options and whether the person you're working with is in your corner.

If you don't have someone in your corner, I hope you take the necessary steps to put everything in place. If you do have someone in your corner, what I share will be an affirmation that you are doing things the right way, you are on the right track, you have the right plan, and you are working with the right people.

I'm thrilled if, after reading this, you have peace of mind in knowing that you are already working with the right people who are doing the right things for you. If not, your peace of mind will come after you understand what you need to do to get things in place or to change what you already have in place.

Bookstores are filled with books about financial products, annuities, stocks, bonds, and details of investments. However, I hope you understand that this is a different kind of book, and I'm on a different kind of mission. This is my way to counter the sales side of the financial industry.

# CHAPTER *ONE*

# People Deserve Better

## DO YOU UNDERSTAND YOUR INVESTMENT STRATEGY?

In my career in the financial services industry, I've spoken with far too many people who don't understand how exactly their investments or strategies work. In addition to not understanding the functionality or the way these investments or products work, they don't understand what these investments are meant to do for them specifically.

Often this means that the product was pitched and sold, perhaps because it has great performance numbers, or simply because the product itself has a great marketing team behind it. Unfortunately, this results in the investment not performing in the way the investor needs it to perform, and many times there can be many such investments in a person's financial portfolio.

There are many ways the folks on Wall Street get you to purchase certain products resulting in complex investments. What has been my experience is that the more complex the investments or strategies get, the less likely the investor is actually benefiting from them. Chances are the only party that is benefiting is the person who sold the product to begin with.

Many people come into my office attempting to explain their complex financial strategies, and they usually fail because they just don't understand them. It's one of the primary reasons why I wholeheartedly believe in educating those that come to see me by taking the time necessary to help people understand.

That's how I serve and give back in this business, unlike many others that are in it merely for themselves. With my approach, I sleep soundly at night knowing I'm making a positive difference in my clients' lives.

## The Industry Creates Complexity

Fifty or sixty years ago, people didn't have access to a lot of readily available information around financial investments. Even thirty or forty years ago, you had to work with a stockbroker and read newspapers to find out how stocks were doing. Today, people have access to more information, and they can learn about investments and strategies quickly.

Unfortunately, to create a market for the people who are selling financial products or working with them, an unnecessary level of complexity was created to combat the readily available information. Over the years, mortgage investments, bond investments, and annuities have grown more complex.

As people have reached for investments to satisfy their comfort levels, whether that is risk or growth, for example, they have reached out for more complex investments, which take many forms.

The insurance industry has complex products ranging from life insurance to long-term care, to annuities, which are extremely complex. The investment world has created elaborate real estate investments tools with internal fees and costs, as well as elaborate investments portfolios. People are reaching for products that they think are going to suit their need, but they simply don't understand how they work.

## With More Complexity Comes Less Understanding

Companies present the benefits or what can be expected from a complex investment but fail to explain how you achieve those benefits. When people don't understand how their investments work, it can harm them. As an example, complex investments typically have a greater amount of risk — whether that's market risk, liquidity risk, or not being able to access money needed in an emergency.

Many people invested a lot of money in technology years ago, and those technology companies were not worth anything. A lot of investors lost almost all, or a great deal of, their life savings because they didn't understand the type of investments they were making.

In addition, when you don't understand your investments, you could be buying something that has incredibly high fees while being in the dark about how those fees are assessed. But, if you don't know what questions to ask in the first place, you are in danger of never knowing how much you are paying in fees for these types of investments. Of course, the higher the fees, the less you are making on that investment.

There are many points to consider when investing, especially when it comes to long-term investing for your retirement. Having complex investments that you don't understand usually results in high risks and high fees. Most importantly, complex investment may not be a fit for what you are trying to accomplish.

## Shiny Object Syndrome

Shiny object syndrome is my tongue-in-cheek term for buying something because it looks and sounds really good. It is usually something that is sold and does not take into consideration all variables required to make a holistic decision. I understand that the function of marketing departments is to sell more, but when we're talking about retirement investments, the sales pitch is focused on how great a particular product appears to be.

But, even when a product looks good on the surface, we may not always know what is going on underneath. You could be pitched a product that appears to be great, which results in your not spending the time to really understand if it is right for you. You need to do your homework, regardless of how bright and shiny the product appears to be.

That homework starts with putting together a plan that includes establishing your goals. You need to ensure that whatever you invest is accomplishing what you want. Only looking on the outside – or merely looking at the shiny packaging of an investment – may not result in your achieving your financial goals.

## ARE YOUR INVESTMENTS TIED TO YOUR GOALS?

Your goals are what unify everything that you need, and they are the reasons why you create a plan. Set and reach for your goals, then you can measure the success of any investment against this initial plan.

Many people plan for retirement by saving money, because that's what they were told to do, without really examining the result.

In the planning process, ask yourself:

- *What are my financial goals?*
- *What do I really need my investments to do for me?*
- *How can I invest to achieve my desired goals?*

Goals are what put everything in motion. If you don't know what your goals are, you will not know how to proceed, who to work with, what you need, and indeed how you are going to accomplish the result you want.

Setting your goals is the most important step. Additionally, if you're not working with someone who is focused on your goals, then you are going to be sold a basket of investments that may be too complex and ultimately will not move you toward achieving what you really want.

Strategies for sound investments include:

1. Discerning what's important to you
2. Defining your goals
3. Working with someone who will:
   - Listen
   - Help you articulate what you want to accomplish
   - Make recommendations

- Put strategies in place to help you achieve your goals

Defining your goals is what will help chart the course for everything that comes after.

## Are You Being Sold?

As with anything, financial companies often have large marketing departments that do their best to make you think it is the greatest investment for you. Add to this situation salespeople whose focus is to sell as much as possible in order to up their commissions, and unsuspecting consumers could be setting themselves up for financial hardship. Many salespeople only know the product they are selling and don't have any knowledge focused on your particular goals and what would be best to achieve them. That's why it's crucial to define your goals and do your homework, particularly when deciding who to work with.

For example, if I need to haul lumber back and forth to a job site, I'm going to need a truck to accomplish that. But, even if a great salesperson sells me a Toyota Prius, that vehicle is not going to do what I need it to do, which is to haul lumber.

The same principle applies to financial investments: *will it help you achieve your goal?*

Be cautious of being pitched and sold.

## Start With the End in Mind

Not starting with the end in mind puts you at risk of merely looking at the here and now. What I mean by that is that you end up looking only at what is doing well, and what you need to accomplish right now.

Starting with the end in mind is another way of establishing your goals down the road, what you want to achieve in the future, and what you need to do to get there. When you define where you want to be in the future, what you want to have, where you want to go, then you can reverse engineer a plan that will get you to that finish line.

Starting with the end means you clearly define where you want to finish and outline a path to get there. For example, if I want to run a marathon in six months, I can then establish a training schedule to ensure I have the best possible chance of success.

Define your goals for retirement, for your legacy. Then, follow your strategies to get there.

## How Best to Define Your Goals

This is a tricky issue because everybody defines their goals differently. For me, defining a goal isn't about earning 10 percent per year, or having a million dollars, or the ability to buy a sports car. To me, defining your goals means defining what you want to achieve or accomplish in your life.

Here are some examples:

- I want to make sure I don't run out of money before I pass away.
- I want to be able to take care of myself if I get sick.
- I want to put my kids through college.
- I want to put my grandkids through college.
- I want to fund a scholarship at the university I attended.
- I want to give money to my church.
- I want to go fishing in the Caribbean every winter.
- I want to travel the world.

These are the types of goals that are worth ensuring you achieve, because they are about a whole, full, and satisfying life.

## A WRITTEN PLAN ENSURES SUCCESS

Having a written plan to achieve your goals is as important as establishing your goals. This written plan becomes the road map that helps you achieve your goals. It helps you move to where you really want to be, manifest your dreams, and defines what you are trying to accomplish. The written plan is what outlines your needs to get where you want to go.

Having a documented written plan puts things into perspective and holds you accountable for ensuring you achieve those goals and dreams. If you have something in writing that indicates how you can achieve your dreams and have everything that you really want, you are more likely to stick with your plan.

You may look down the road and think: *this is what I want, and here is what I think I need to do to get there.*

However, if you haven't written down your plan, you may tend to not pay attention and your plan will eventually slip from your mind. At the very least, you may not achieve what you want as quickly as you anticipated.

In an ideal world, everybody in the financial industry would work with people to develop a plan before recommending an investment or product. But, unfortunately, that tends not to be the case with many financial advisors. As a result, some people that come to see me are confused, some feel that they have everything under control, and some feel that they are never going to reach their goals.

Putting together a plan that will ensure you can achieve what you really want—a plan that outlines exactly what needs to be done—is really the only way to make sure you have success in the long run.

**Facts and Figures**

I am a Certified Financial Planner practitioner, and I always read the surveys completed by the Certified Financial Planner Board of Standards. This survey, conducted in 2012, clearly shows how most people do not have a financial plan in place for their retirement.

[Reprinted with permission. 2012 Household Financial Planning Survey, A Summary of Key Findings, July 23, 2012. Prepared for: Certified Financial Planner Board of Standards, Inc. and the Consumer Federation of America. Prepared by: Princeton Survey Research Associates International. Please follow this link for the complete report: cfp.net/docs/news-events---research-facts-figures/2012_household_financial_planning_survey.pdf?sfvrsn=2]

When asked if they were implementing a plan to meet savings goals in six specific areas, about two-thirds (65%) of decision-makers say they follow a plan for at least one of their savings goals. This compares with only 31 percent who say they have ever prepared a comprehensive financial plan—or used a professional to prepare one—that includes things like savings and investments, retirement planning, and insurance needs.

Planning is most often reported for saving for one's retirement. As many as half (49%) of non-retirees say they have begun saving for retirement and follow a plan or schedule for how often, how much, and where they are saving or investing for this purpose. Since the 1990s, trends in workplace retirement benefits have shifted away from pensions and other vehicles where the employer makes all decisions toward 401(k) and similar retirement plans where employees make direct contributions and decisions themselves. The survey found a significant increase in how many of those enrolled in 401(k) or similar plans make annual contributions (77% vs. 66%). Despite this positive trend, the number of non-retirees who say they have a plan in place to invest for retirement is essentially unchanged (49% vs. 51% in 1997).

As might be expected, those with higher incomes are more likely to plan. Over half (55%) of those with household incomes of $100,000 or more have a comprehensive plan, compared with roughly a third (35%) of in the $50,000–$99,999 bracket, and a quarter (25%) of those in the $25,000-$49,999 bracket. Such plans are a rarity among those with incomes lower than $25,000 (10%).

Planning Benefits all Income Levels, not Just the Wealthy

The benefits of a comprehensive financial plan are further demonstrated by the smart saving and money management practices associated with it. For those at higher income levels, planners put more of their income into savings than non-planners and report having built greater wealth. For example, planners with incomes of $50,000-$99,999 are more likely than non-planners to say they save 10 percent of their income or more (57% vs. 39%) and to have accumulated at least $100,000 in investments so far (37% vs. 19%). Similar differences are found between planners and non-planners in the $100,000 or more income bracket.

Financial planning is often seen as a tool for the more affluent, but the survey provides strong evidence that those with modest incomes also benefit. Families with fewer financial resources are most vulnerable to credit card debt spiraling out of control. Having a financial plan is associated with handling credit card bills in a way that minimizes risk of credit card debt problems. Among those in the $25,000–$49,999 income category, 46 percent of those with a plan say they usually pay their credit card bill in full each month, compared with 26 percent of non-planners. The margin is 41 percent to 16 percent between planners and non-planners in the under $25,000 category.

The number of people that have a written plan is a staggering low number. It's not difficult to create, it's something that everybody needs, but the number of people that have one is low. Approximately one third of the population has a plan which means that two thirds do not.

Putting a plan in place becomes the most important step, and these facts and figures back that up. Many American households have seen decreases in income, combined with too much debt, leaving them unable to save.

There are also those who are confident and started saving when they were young; they have a written financial plan, which they created with the end goal in mind. They have defined their goals and they have invested appropriately to achieve those goals over time.

## Your Written Plan Is Your Roadmap

If I want to drive from Jacksonville, Florida to Nashville, Tennessee, I need a map. I need something that's going to show me what roads to take, what turns to make, and when. Our retirement goals are no different. We need a map to outline how we are going to get where we want to go.

That means we must first define where we want to be, and then we can put together the steps that we need to take to get there. For some people, this is as simple as changing an investment strategy; some people may need to work longer; still others may need to put aside more money.

The roadmap is what will allow you to know what you need to do to get the result that you seek.

## Monitor and Measure Your Plan

Having a written plan gives you something that you can review and follow, but it doesn't stop there. You need to constantly update that plan — your road map — and you need to measure it against where you are expected to be at any particular point.

This measurement is how you know if anything needs to be done differently, if any roads need to be taken that you weren't thinking about when you originally wrote your plan. You must measure where you are presently with your timeline and end goal.

If you're not monitoring and updating your plan, you are not measuring yourself, which could lead to completely missing the mark—your intended end goal. In the financial and retirement worlds, the reality is that everything that affects us is constantly changing.

Our healthcare laws, prospectuses, investments, and tax laws are changing. Legal documents also need to be changed, but, most importantly, what changes even more is people.

Maybe your goals have changed. Maybe what you are trying to accomplish has changed, and the plan that you originally put in place needs to be amended. That's why you must monitor, measure, and update your plan to ascertain if your original goals are still valid, and to establish new goals that align with your life changes.

# CHAPTER *TWO*

# Retirement Planning Is More Than Your Investments

## INVESTMENTS ARE A MEANS TO AN END

Our lives are more than the things that are in them. Our dreams and what we do for others often require money, some type of income. Our investments can help us accomplish our goals, live our dreams, and do for our loved ones.

Unfortunately, too many people view investments as the focus in their lives instead of using the investments to achieve their goals, to do what they really want in their lives. When it comes to retirement planning, I talk to too many people who merely concentrate on a basket of investments, instead of what those investments can help them achieve in life.

We all have dreams, we all have goals, we all have things that we want to do, and investments — money — are what we need to achieve them. But money is not the most important element in our lives.

We all need money, and we all need a source of income to live. We need savings and investments to retire. Investments can provide a stable income to stay retired. To fulfill our dreams and goals, we need to look at every aspect of our lives.

We spend our entire lives working and saving money so that one day we no longer need to work. We want time to enjoy other activities in life. Our investments are what get us there, not the whole reason, and not the whole focus. It's what allows us to live that life and live those dreams.

## Grandma's Story

My grandmother and my parents have influenced me a great deal. But, when it comes to the world of finance, my grandmother has been the primary influence. She handled most of the finances in her family. She inherited money when she was young, and she did all the investing. So, when I was young and learning about the financial world, she and I would have a lot of talks about investment strategies, what stocks to buy, how to invest over time, how dividends and interest work, and all the inner workings of investments.

Shortly after my grandfather passed away, she and I would take trips after the holidays. She would come visit my family in Jacksonville, Florida, and then she and I would get in the car and go visit my uncle. On one of those trips she turned to me and said how much she hated the way she handled the family finances.

That struck me as odd because I thought she did a wonderful job of investing. She was a great investor, she saved a lot of money, she invested over time, and she did very well. She raised her family. She put kids through school, she put the grandkids through school, and I wanted to know what she meant by that.

She told me the story about a house that they wanted to buy. She didn't want to use the savings she had set aside to buy it, and it was more than they wanted to spend on my grandfather's salary. What struck me was that as successful as she had been in investing, it was a missed lifestyle opportunity that was one of her big regrets fifty years later. She had given up the opportunity to live in the house of her choice simply because she hadn't wanted to use her money to purchase it.

That experience taught me that this business, this world of retirement planning and finance, has more to do with people's goals and how they want to live their lives than just the money.

**Her Influence**

That story made me realize that this business is more about what money needs to do *for* people. This realization was a catalyst that led to my studies to become a certified financial planner. After much research, I discovered that certified financial planning was a much more holistic and broad approach that looked at many things, not just investments.

Financial planning looks at peoples' lives, coming up with a plan rather than just having a basket of products, or a portfolio of stocks and bonds. It looks at the person, and starts with creating goals.

In addition to investments, financial planning looks at taxes, at estate planning, at healthcare, and how to do the best for a client while looking at their entire lives, rather than just looking at the money they have. Peoples' lives are more than just their investments.

**What Has Not Having a Team Cost You?**

I regularly review people's portfolios, investments, and savings. I often see parts that could be done better, or differently, if the items were looked at together. I try to look at all the individual pieces of the puzzle as a whole. This is why holistic financial planning is so important; decisions must be made in light of everything, not just one piece at a time.

Having a team of people that examine, analyze, and strategically position your investments to best achieve your goals often means you are going to be more successful. It could mean you have more money. It could mean you have tax savings, but, most importantly, it could mean the difference between helping your grandchildren or not, or taking an extra long vacation, or being able to fund a scholarship.

Working with a team that looks at everything together is always better than merely looking at one piece of the puzzle.

## WHAT DO YOU WANT YOUR INVESTMENTS TO DO FOR YOU?

To me, that question differs from asking what you want your investments to do. What you want your investments to do includes wanting them to grow and create income.

However, I want you to look at your investments from the standpoint of what you want them to do for you:

- What do you want to do in retirement?

- What are your dreams?

- What are your goals?

- Where do you want to be in five years? Ten years? Twenty years?

- What do you want to be doing in five years? Are you sitting at home waiting for the kids and the grandkids to come visit or are you traveling the world?

- Are you philanthropically inclined, giving money to your church or to a charity?

- What do need your money to do for you?

If you focus on what you need your money to do *for* you, you can have that road map that you created. You can make sure your investments are strategically placed and structured in a way that you can achieve your goals. By that I mean not merely the goal of having a certain amount of money, but your desire to contribute to a charity that is near and dear to your heart, or your wish to travel the world. That's what your money needs to do for you rather than what your money needs to do.

For my grandparents, that meant being able to leave money for the family as an enduring legacy. Even though they have been gone for a long time, in times of emergency and when financial help was needed, my parents have been able to help out, and it was understood that the money came from our grandparents. This reinforces my grandparents' original desire to share and to give to their family.

This legacy has a profound impact. I'm certain that somewhere they are smiling and comforted by the fact that they accomplished what they set out to do with their financial resources. Their memory lives on, and that is one of the most important things about investments. It's not just about having the bucket of money, it's about doing what you really dream of doing with that bucket of money.

**Travel**

Many of us do our best to save money so that one day we no longer need to work. Instead, we enjoy spending that money we've earned. A popular way to spend money is by traveling and seeing different parts of the world. During our working lives, our travel opportunities may be limited to two or three weeks at a time, but once we retire, time is no longer a restriction. We can choose to explore other parts of the world, or other parts of the country.

Retirement is the perfect time to experience other cultures, experiment with different cuisines, and get to know more about the people of the world. As I said, it is one of the top desires and what people save for most of their lives.

While I'm still working, I'm one of those people that can only travel for two weeks at a time. I'd love to be able to go somewhere, stay longer periods of time, and really immerse myself in the local cultures. I think that is something that I share with a lot of people.

Some people may want to get in an RV and travel across the country; some people may want to get on a plane and spend a month in Europe. Some people may want to go the Far East or the Caribbean or South America or Africa and see the wildlife in the Serengeti National Park. Whatever travel adventure you wish to take, your financial plan can help you get there.

**Family**

For a lot of people in retirement, they want enough money to be able to help and take care of their family. This could include anything from the freedom to visit often, particularly if the grandchild lives in another city, to buying gifts.

For my grandmother, it was important for her to help all her grandchildren with their college education. She set money aside for each of her grandchildren to be able to go to school, as she had done with her own children.

Giving to family, helping support their dreams and their desires is something that I see a great deal, as is leaving a legacy. Leaving a financial legacy ensures that you will always be remembered. For example, I remember my grandfather giving me a big hug followed by our special handshake, which always resulted in him passing me a few dollars when our palms met. It may not have been a lot of money, but to a seven-year-old kid or to a teenager, it meant the world.

Being able to give back to family is one of the most important things that I see in just about everybody that I speak with regularly.

**Giving**

Giving back is another goal for a lot of people, because we naturally want to give back to the people or places that have given us so much. Philanthropy in all its different forms is a wonderful trait and, to me, is incredibly admirable.

Many clients give back to their primary schools, their high schools, their colleges or universities, or their church. Donating is one of the things that I try to help shepherd and foster when a client demonstrates an interest in giving back.

Most people want to make sure that they have enough for themselves, but they also build into their budget a weekly tithe to their church or a gift to fund a scholarship. Others honor their educational institution by giving back.

## ORGANIZING YOUR TEAM

To be truly successful, we need other people around us for support. Even in solo sports like tennis, players have coaches and trainers — people that surround them to help them be successful when then step on the court. The President of the United States is not going to be successful on his own. He needs a cabinet, advisors, and others that do a myriad of things to make sure his time in office is successful and to make sure the country is thriving.

I would not be able to write this book without the help of those that help me think about what I want to convey, ignite creative thoughts and ideas from within me, and guide me in sharing about myself on the page. The same holds true for our retirement planning and financial investments. You can't do it alone. You need to have a team of people — working together as one — that will help make you successful and make sure that your goals are achieved.

You may think that you don't need a team, but there are basic items that must be put into place for success. No matter how much money you have saved, you need a team to help you achieve your goals. So, whether you have thirty million dollars or thirty thousand dollars, you will need input from more than one person.

No one person can wear all the hats. No one person can do everything that you need. Having a team, making sure that you are communicating your needs, and ensuring that everybody is working toward your goals is vital.

## The Sum Is Bigger Than the Parts

All the individual team members play an important role. However, ultimate success is achieved when there is organization; when team members work towards a common, unified goal; when they talk to one another; and when they work with one another rather than each person working individually and not truly being part of the team.

In business, it takes many people fulfilling different roles to achieve one successful goal. The same thing applies in government, in sports, and in any successful endeavor. You need everybody working together, not just individuals working on their own.

## The Team Needs to Know Goals

As important as it is to have all the necessary people on your team, you also need to have them all focus on your goals:

- What are you really trying to accomplish?
- What do you need?
- What do you want to have happen?

Any decision that you make is going to have an effect or some type of repercussion on the other. You need to have everybody on the same page so that everybody knows the impact of each choice, and you can make the most informed decision possible.

In the financial world, most investment decisions are going to have some type of taxable consequence. Your portfolio, your savings, your goals and desires, and how you wish your investments to be passed on might need the input of an attorney in the form of estate planning.

Your health care cost could also be affected by the amount of money that you earn. There are all sorts of examples along those lines where everybody needs to be talking to one another so they understand what you want to have happen, what you need to have happen, and what they need to do to make the best decisions to help you achieve your goals.

# CHAPTER *THREE*

# Your Team Members

## ACCOUNTANT/TAX PROFESSIONAL

We work with accountants because we want to make sure that we are paying our fair share to our government for the services they provide. One of the accountants that I work with very closely has a favorite saying: *Render to Caesar that which is Caesars' but don't give him any more.* I think that is important to do, but we want to work with an accountant for another reason.

We want to look at what is the most efficient way to pay our fair share, but not right now — we want to consider the future. So, taxes are one of the most important and financially scary things that everybody faces, but we all know we must pay them. We want to make sure that we do it properly and efficiently over the remainder of our lives, and, if possible, our children's and grandchildren's lives.

Death and taxes are the two things that are certain in life, and you can't avoid either. However, we can try to minimize the effect that taxes are going to have on our lives, on the lives of our children, and on the lives of our grandchildren in the best possible way.

This means that when it comes to your retirement planning, we should involve an accountant. We must look at our decisions while keeping their taxable consequences in mind, and search for the smartest, most efficient way to handle those tax decisions. That means having a CPA on your team who's going to look out for what you are doing right now, and what you will be doing in the future.

**Tax Planning versus Tax Preparation**

To me, there's a big difference between tax planning and tax preparation. Tax preparation is what most of us think of when we think about taxes. It is, to me, the art of looking at where we are right now and then looking backward, making sure that we took all the exemptions into account; making sure that we included all our deductions and claimed all our income. It also means that we have accounted for all our assets properly, and that the tax forms are properly completed so we avoid an audit. We need to pay our share.

Tax planning, on the other hand, is the art of looking where we are right now and looking forward. It's figuring out how we pay the least in taxes possible, not just this year, but also every year over the course of our lives. That's an important thing to do because sometimes it may involve paying a little more in taxes now to save a little later. Sometimes it means doing things exactly the way we currently are, but we always want to look forward and try and project how to minimize taxes over the remainder of our lives and our children's lives.

## The Ever-Changing Tax Code

I think we can all agree that over the last fifty years — even over the last five years — that the tax laws and the code of our tax system have changed drastically. As I write this, the people in Washington are gearing up for what they are calling a major tax reform. We have seen this before, and we will see it again.

As Benjamin Franklin said, "In this world nothing can be said to be certain, except death and taxes."

Over the last several years, there have been over five thousand changes to our tax code. If you look at the amount of debt that our country carries right now, most people believe that our taxes are going to be changing in the future. Taxes change and the only control we have is who we vote for to be in control of the tax law. We do the best with what we know right now, but we also understand that things will be changing in the future.

Because many people think their taxes will be going up, we need to look at where we are right now and make the best decisions for our financial plan moving forward.

So, the question is how do we minimize our taxes over the remainder of our life in light of the changing tax code?

It's something that we absolutely must consider because being efficient with our taxes can mean the difference between being able to do what we want or not.

**Tax Planning Over Multiple Generations**

Tax planning over multiple generations is pretty simple:

*How do I minimize taxes, not just over my life, but also over the lives of my loved ones once I'm gone?*

Different types of assets are going to have different types of qualifications. For an example, a traditional individual retirement account (IRA) is going to be taxable no matter who takes it out. If I take it out, I must pay taxes on it. If I pass it on to my children, my children will have to pay taxes on it, and so on. There could be a way to pass an IRA on to a charity, and qualified charities are tax-exempt.

Assets that I pass along, such as a home or a stock, are going to have a different tax treatment if I pass them on to my children, my grandchildren, or to a charity. Life insurance benefit proceeds are tax free.

Here are some of the questions an accountant will help you answer:

- What types of assets do you have?
- How are they titled?
- What is the tax treatment when you pass assets to you children or grandchildren?
- What is the tax treatment when you pass assets to a charity?

That's why determining what you want and what your goals are is so important in the world of taxes as it relates to a legacy. I may want to pass on a type of asset to a charity while leaving another to my child. Or, perhaps it's a matter of replacing the taxable asset with a tax-free asset.

That's what the art of planning and looking forward rather than looking backward will help you fine-tune, and it's one of the most vital considerations when it comes to leaving money over multiple generations.

## ATTORNEY

An attorney belongs on our team because at some point we need to make sure that our investments and assets get passed on to whom we choose, whether a husband or wife, children or grandchildren, a beloved charity, or a combination. In most cases, this means we need a legal document that stipulates how our assets are to be allocated. An attorney is the person that drafts those documents and makes sure that in the eyes of the law we have everything properly titled or properly directed.

An attorney is one of the primary team members. The estate law — the laws that govern the allocation of assets and how we are protected during our lives — is something that constantly changes, like the tax code. Just as our estate value and estate taxes change, so too do the rules within each state change.

We need to make sure that there is someone at the table who is advising us on matters of change within the documents that we have created. Also, as our lives, goals, and priorities change, to whom and how we distribute our assets may change as well. So, we need to make sure that an estate-planning attorney is involved.

It's important to have an attorney at the table with our other team members because as the value of our assets change, they may need to become more involved. For example, there may be tax ramifications or other issues that need attorney consultations. An attorney has a primary role and is an important member of your team.

## Efficiency

Many of us spend a lifetime saving money or accumulating things of value such as real estate and property, stocks and bonds, automobiles, or jewelry. We may want a piece of artwork to go to a nephew or a niece, and we want to make sure this is done as efficiently as possible.

If we do not have a plan or have documents in place that specify where each item goes, our desires for allocation are unknown. If you don't have your own plan, the government steps in to plan on your behalf, and your assets and possessions may not be distributed in the way that you would have liked.

We want our assets and items of value to go to our loved ones as efficiently as possible. We want as little government intervention as possible. Most importantly, we want to be in charge of the allocation of our assets. Having a plan in place that's been vetted by an attorney ensures that the court system is avoided as it relates to estate planning.

## Fees and Costs

Depending on how we pass things to our families or to the next generation, it can have an impact on what types of fees the recipients pay. For example, in Florida when a person passes away and assets go to probate, loved ones can't just walk up and deal with probate court themselves — they must hire an attorney.

Probate attorneys, of course, charge a fee. In addition, court costs will apply. But, this must be done for assets to be allocated to loved ones.

Proper estate planning can ensure that you create proper documentation and living trusts that will establish the structure needed to avoid probate. A small fee may be required to work through this process, but it will mean avoiding much bigger fees for your children and your grandchildren down the road. This helps preserve the integrity and the overall value of your estate.

Proper estate planning could also help minimize taxes, depending on the size of the estate that you are passing along. Having an attorney at the table, along with an accountant or CPA, is just as important because there are tax ramifications that can be taken into consideration with regards to your estate planning.

## Protecting Your Interests During Your Life

Effectively and efficiently passing assets to the next generation during the estate planning process is not the only reason to have an attorney at the table. There are documents and other components that we need to take care of to preserve our interests while we are alive.

For example, if I am hospitalized due to a head injury, I need somebody in place to make financial decisions on my behalf. There could be a need for this person to access my accounts, take money out of my IRA, or file my taxes. If I am incapacitated, I need to give someone the legal authority to handle those financial matters on my behalf. I would need a durable power of attorney.

If I am incapacitated and healthcare decisions need to be made — for example, a surgical procedure is required — I need someone to authorize that procedure. This means I need a separate healthcare document — a healthcare power of attorney — to be in place for this to happen.

While it's important to have an estate-planning attorney working on our behalf to ensure our assets are allocated according to our wishes after we pass, it's equally important to have an attorney available to ensure the proper documents are in place to protect our interests during life.

## HOLISTIC FINANCIAL PLANNER AND INVESTMENT MANAGER

For a comfortable retirement, most of us need more than what our social security and pension will provide. We need money set aside, and the investments that we have worked hard for, that we have saved for, are going to allow us to do the things that we want to do in retirement.

We have talked about the importance of working with someone who takes a holistic approach to your financial planning. Having them advise on investments is critical to achieving your goals. It's not merely about making money or achieving a certain rate of return. It's about being able to afford to retire and making sure we don't run out of money before we pass away. It could also be about leaving money for our children's and our grandchildren's educations. We need someone who is going to help guide us through the jungle of investing to make sure that we are successful.

On this topic, I am not mentioning specifics about the pros and cons of a variable versus a fixed annuity, or which stock is better than another, or how to buy a bond. There are numerous books and plenty of places that you can find information about those specific questions you may have about investments.

Instead, I want to focus on what you are currently doing, in general. I want to focus on making sure that you are taking only the risk necessary to achieve your goals. Choosing the correct stocks, bonds, and interest bearing accounts are an important part of any portfolio, but what those investments do together to achieve those goals is crucial. A financial advisor will make sure that they are analyzed with respect to what you are doing currently and then tie everything together to achieve your goals.

## Examine What You're Doing Currently

Investment is an area in which the advice differs when you are working and saving. When you are accumulating, you know that you need to save, and there are a lot of people who can give advice on this aspect.

The situation changes as you get closer to retirement, and you need that money to start being more protected. You need to be protected from loss, and you also need it to be generating income.

You may retire with a pile of money, but to stay retired you need the income that money can provide. So, examining what you are doing currently is something that everybody absolutely needs to do.

Some current actions that should be examined:

- Evaluate how much risk you are taking right now because most people are taking more risk than they probably should.
- Evaluate how much income your portfolio and your savings generate.
- Evaluate the fees you are paying.

A myriad of issues need to be analyzed and examined constantly to make sure that your money is going to be protected and be safe and invested appropriately to achieve your goals.

**The Goals Your Investments Need to Achieve**

When creating your financial plan, you must start with your goals when it comes to your investments. Your goals will determine the type of investments you need, how aggressive they need to be, or how conservative they need to be. Goals will determine whether you need stocks and bonds, annuities, or a combination.

If you know where you need to wind up the road map, the investment strategy will automatically fall in line. Don't just pick an investment strategy and hope that you make it to the finish line. If you start with the finish line in mind, you can custom tailor strategies that are going to give you the highest probability of success with the least amount of risk to achieve it. That is what I mean about starting with the end in mind.

I gave an example earlier about running a marathon, but imagine another scenario. I want to take a trip to Barbados next year, and it's going to cost me ten thousand dollars. I currently don't have any money saved. I know that I need to start saving to be able to take that trip. The same thing applies for investing. If you know what your goal is, you can then custom tailor the investment portfolio to make sure you achieve it.

I remember looking at the Christmas catalog as a kid and seeing an item I really wanted. If it cost fifty dollars, I knew I would have to mow the lawn a certain number of times to accumulate the necessary money to purchase it. I didn't just mindlessly mow the lawn, set aside the money, and then say, "Oh, look I can buy this now." If I knew what I needed to do to gain the item in question, it became easy for me to achieve it.

## Only Take as Much Risk as You Need

All investments involve some measure of risk. It may be stock market risk, it may be interest rate risk, or it may be inflation risk. Avoiding risk is next to impossible—you must deal with the risks in front of you. Not everybody needs to take large risks when it comes to investing.

Usually when we think of risk, we think of stock market risk. We believe to grow our money we must invest aggressively, or we should invest in stocks. This option could potentially mean that your investment could go down in value.

For most people, the potential of earning an extra 1, 2, or 3 percent per year with higher risk investments isn't going to change their lives. However, if this higher risk investment doesn't do well, it could mean they would lose a substantial portion more. They may lose 10, 20, or 40 percent. To be sure, losing that money would indeed impact their lives.

Some people who can withstand the downside that a high-risk investment can produce, have found themselves in fortunate situations. Being in this position can be a wonderful place to be, because it gives them the opportunity to manage risks accordingly, or take even more risks than the average person can comfortably take.

But not everyone is in a position to withstand the downside potential of a high-risk investment and still do the things that they ultimately want to do.

A properly developed investment plan should help you manage the behavior that leads people to make poor investment decisions based on emotion. It allows you to take risk when appropriate, but to be an investor, not a speculator. Earmarking investments for specific needs can help with this planning. It isn't just about taking too much, or too little risk; it is about managing it appropriately through planning.

Again, that is why you must start with the end in mind. That is why you need to make sure that what you are doing currently is in line with your long-term goals so that you can manage the amount of risk you are taking. Only take as much risk as you need.

# CHAPTER *FOUR*

# Everyone's Situation Is Different

## WHEN YOU'RE A HAMMER, EVERYTHING LOOKS LIKE A NAIL

This traditional saying is one of my favorites. It applies in this industry because there are many different people that hold themselves out to be financial planners. There are many titles in this industry as well: financial advisors, financial planners, wealth managers, and brokers.

They all hold themselves out to be one thing, but too often they are not. They do one thing and one thing only. They are specialists or trained in one discipline, process, or sales strategy, along with their peers, and that is all their firm focuses on. Unfortunately, it becomes their solution to everything.

Advisors that present themselves as financial planners can mislead many investors. These advisors only offer narrowly focused advice or a single product solution that is not really a solution at all or in your best interest.

I'll talk more about what that means for a few different groups here as we move forward.

The bottom line is that instead of working with someone who is focused on just one area, it's best to deal with a true financial planner who looks at a lot of different places for a complete financial picture. The practice of financial planning must involve a lot more than just one narrow focus of concentration.

A study from Surely and Associates revealed in 2013 over 166,000 advisors claimed that they provided a financial planning focused practice. It was determined, however, that only 38 percent of them actually provided true financial planning services.[1]

There are a lot of people out there who try to present themselves as financial planners but it is only their title that pronounces them as such. These include stockbrokers; life insurance or annuities sales people; 401(k) advisors, registered representatives, or captive agents. There is a need and a push for additional regulatory standards.

The American consumer is looking for these standards to be in place, and it is something that you deserve. You expect certain standards to be met by doctors, lawyers,

---

1    cfp.net/news-events/lates-news/2014/10/20/amid-surge-in-demand-for-financial-planners-consumers-are-harmed-by-lack-of-appropriate-regulatory-standards

and accountants. You should expect your financial planner to have a level of expertise as well.

One of the reasons I worked so hard to acquire and maintain my certified financial planner (CFP®) certification is because I wanted to demonstrate that I had the necessary expertise. I also think it holds distinction. It is important for people to feel confident that the person they are working with is truly going to provide them with a planning service, rather than just a sales pitch or a focus in one area only.

## The Insurance Agent

This is one group of people who often call themselves financial advisors, financial planners, or wealth managers. The truth is, they work for an insurance company, or their practice or business focuses only on insurance-based solutions. A lot of times, this takes the place of life insurance or annuities sales people.

If you were to meet with this person, and you presented them with all your retirement goals and your financial needs, their recommendations would be insurance-based — and that's all this person can offer you. While insurance solutions are not bad when they are used properly and as part of a bigger plan, they are not appropriate for your entire financial plan. Insurance is not the solution to everything for everybody.

As mentioned, an insurance agent's focus is insurance, and it's likely the only expertise they hold; they are not licensed to provide any other type of product. Because an insurance agent is only able to provide one solution, you need a broader solution to meet all your financial goals. You need to look at options that offer you multiple solutions, not merely a single answer. That's the way retirement planning should be.

## The Registered Representative / Stockbroker

Stockbrokers have been around for a long time. Back when I was a kid, one could call a stockbroker and they were likely to say, "I have a hot stock tip!"

They made recommendations and bought stock on your behalf. Then you read about your particular stock in the paper to see how it was performing over time.

A registered representative is a registered advisor or registered broker who represents a particular company and provides investment advice. Again, these types of advisors focus on stock and bond based investments, or investor managed accounts, and they typically are employees of large companies or corporations.

Their financial obligation is to the company they work for, the company's management staff, and shareholders. They have a standard of care that is called *the suitability standard of care*. They are required to offer you something that is a suitable investment based on your goals or your risk tolerance. However, their suggestion may not necessarily be the best thing for you, but merely suitable.

The U.S. Department of Labor is working hard to implement rules requiring anyone who provides advice to be held to a higher standard. This is something that is starting to change in the industry with the introduction of the fiduciary level of care. This means that your best interests must always be the focus. So, instead of offering something that is suitable but at the same time might be expensive or a proprietary investment offered by the company that I work for, I need to offer you the best alternative, even if it means the guy down the street has the best option for you.

That is the big difference between someone who acts as a fiduciary and someone who is a registered representative or a captive agent who does not hold to a fiduciary standard.

**The Dabbler**

Years ago, I was working with clients who were in the medical field. They said that they wanted to make changes to their retirement accounts because of investment advice that they had received from a colleague. This colleague had worked in the medical field but also had managed his own retirement accounts, and he was giving investment advice to his peers and other work colleagues.

It is easy to take advice from someone that you perceive to be successful. Often, people will brag about their investment performance, how well they did in a stock, or how wonderful they have done in some other area of finance.

But, is it wise to take advice and recommendations based on another person's goals and personal road map — particularly when financial planning isn't their area of expertise?

Their suggestions may work out for you, but are you certain it is the best solution for you?

Are there other products and options that are more beneficial for your situation and goals?

A CFP® practitioner is in the best position to advise and make recommendations based on your personal interests and goals.

## YOU'VE TRAVELED A UNIQUE PATH

In over twenty years of working with clients and sharing with them a little of my story but, more importantly, learning about theirs, I have come to realize that no two people arrive where they are by taking the same path. The journey to retirement and through retirement is different for everybody. Couples with no children will take a different route than large families, for example, because everyone does things a little bit differently.

You may have worked at a job for forty-five years, retired, received a gold watch and retirement party, then receive a check for the rest of your life. Or, you may have bounced from job to job, from state to state, and country to country requiring you to accumulate your savings and wealth in a different manner.

The point is at some point most of us want to stop working entirely, or at least cut back, which means we are going to need to rely on our savings, or on all the things that we have done until that point to get us to and through retirement.

How you arrive at retirement is unique—and it's wonderful to hear so many different stories—but this uniqueness is also what presents the need for individual, customized planning to make sure that the rest of your journey can continue as well as what you did to arrive in the first place.

Everyone is different, of course. Everyone's goals and needs are different. How you got to retirement is going to inform your opinions and decision-making on everything you do moving forward.

You may be more conservative with your investments by nature, or you may be more aggressive with your investments by nature. You may have your lifestyle costs covered by guaranteed sources of income, such as social security and pensions, and you may not need to dip into your savings. Or, you may want to give all your savings to your family or your beloved charity.

Ensuring that your goals are achieved is where the planner enters the picture, as he or she makes sure that your path and your legacy are cared for.

## Pensions

I am in my forties. I have worked in the private sector for most of my life and will not have a pension. My father worked in the private sector for most of his life, and he does have a bit of a pension, as does my mom.

Pensions are something that used to be much more popular. It was a way to recruit and retain good quality employees. Companies wanted to keep employees around, and it was a benefit that basically said: *if you work for us for a certain amount of time, when you retire, we are going to give you a check every month for the rest of your life.*

Pensions are a wonderful security blanket, a wonderful foundation to have. Some companies provided pension options that also covered spouses during that period.

But pensions are now disappearing. Pensions are much less popular now than they were sixty, seventy, eighty, ninety years ago — even twenty or thirty years ago.

With the advent of the 401(k) and retirement plans, it's become less expensive for most companies to be able to offer matching contributions to these retirement plans. In addition, society has become more transient — we don't stay at one job for thirty years or longer, or even twenty years. We move from job to job to job, and sometimes all around the country, or all around the world, and we need to accumulate money on our own through the 401(k) plan, 403(b) plans, or through matching contributions from employers.

Pensions are wonderful, and if you have one through your employer, that's great. However, it needs to be evaluated. Sometimes you can do better on your own than what an employer can offer you on a pension option. You need to understand how your company's pension option works and how it fits into your overall retirement plan.

The potential for the loss of income due to the pensioner's passing also needs to be looked at and reviewed.

Like I said, having a pension is great but what happens if that pension goes away and you have been relying on it for income?

**Inherited Assets**

The largest transfer of wealth in our country has yet to occur. It is starting as parents of baby boomers age and pass away. The largest generation of people in our country is retiring, and they have been saving with retirement plans and 401(k)s for many decades. They have accumulated a great deal of wealth.

This wealth is going to be passed from generation to generation. People are going to have more and more money; therefore, they will need sound advice. They will need advice on what this money can do for them over the remainder of their lives, as well as guidance for the money that is going to be passed along in a legacy.

We also need to look at life expectancy, goals, and long-term planning for the people that are in line to inherit. Additionally, recommendations can be made for how people receive the inheritance. For example, some people may not be mature enough to receive large inheritances. This means that you may need to put controls in place to make sure young people do not blow through the money or spend it in ways that you deem unacceptable.

Many people who have inherited from their parents will be passing assets along to their children and to their grandchildren. This process requires a certain level of planning and a certain level of specification to ensure that the money is being used in the right ways, and that your wishes and your parents' wishes are taken into consideration as well.

## Savings

Savings are a cornerstone. To me, saving money is something that we all need to do when we are working. We need to be putting money away in some way, whether that is through our retirement plan, a 401(k), an IRA, or money in the bank.

It is something we all need to do because one day we may not have the ability to earn a paycheck, or we may not want to work to earn a paycheck. We will need to rely on the money that we set aside to fill the gap.

There are certain things in our system that are going to be provided to us, such as social security, that will help the foundation of our retirement income. But we need income above and beyond that, and that money comes from our savings or from other options that we have accumulated during our lives. Saving is something that we all know we need to do.

## YOUR UNIQUE IDEAS FOR YOUR FUTURE

Close your eyes and imagine for moment your perfect retirement.

What does it look like?

You need to set the stage and figure out what is most important to you. Everyone is going to want something different. What I want for my retirement is going to be completely different from what my coworkers want or what my brothers and sisters want.

Your goal may be buying a tiny little bungalow on the beach, or it may be traveling as much as you can across the world. Whatever you want is unique to you, and it is based on your experience, on what you want for your family and for yourself.

Although some people may want some similar things, such as travel, the details are going to be different for everyone. I know many people love cruises, but I'm not one of them. I want to fly to my destination and then park myself on a beach, or sit outside my bungalow reading a book in a hammock.

It's going to be different for everybody. You should look at what you really want out of your retirement. It is my job as a financial planner to help you figure out how you can do whatever is on your wish list. This is the essence of your dreams.

Five years from now, where are you and what are you doing?

What do I have to do as your advisor to make sure that five years from now you are doing exactly that?

Ten years from now, are you doing exactly what you want?

That is where the financial advisor fits in— understanding what you want for the future and helping you create a road map to get there. My job is not about stocks, bonds, or annuities. I want to make sure that your dreams are achieved, not your investments. I take care of the investments so that you reach your desired goals.

**Traveling**

I love to travel, but I don't get to do as much of it as I would like. When I discuss retirement plans with people, traveling is often at the top of their wish list— it's what they want to do with the next chapter of their lives, and it's what they have dreamed of for some time.

Clients also love to share with me the travel adventures they have already taken. I love to hear the stories of where people have been and where they are planning on going next—they give me ideas for where I should go the next time I plan a vacation.

My brother is fortunate enough to have a job that gives him lengthy periods of time off in between contracts and in between working hours. He can go on two to three week trips while only taking a few vacation days, and he takes full advantage of it. He's traveled the world and will continue to do so.

Traveling may be one of the goals you have for your retirement. If so, it needs to be built into your plan because it is something that has a cost associated with it. Traveling, depending on your destination of choice, can be quite expensive.

If traveling is on your agenda for your retirement, think about where you want to go ahead of time. Think about what you have spent on past vacations and make sure that you budget for the trips you wish to take when you are in the planning stage.

Most of us want to travel and we want to fit as much travel in as we can shortly after retirement while we are still in our fifties, sixties, or seventies. As we get older, we may be more comfortable staying home and relaxing instead of being on the go and active, which is typical when one is traveling. Build your travel plans into your retirement road map, focus on making sure that you can afford it, and go see the world.

## Staying at Home and Visiting with Family

Traveling is not the be-all and end-all for everybody. A lot of people have had the opportunity to travel the world while they were younger, or maybe their business or work involved a lot of traveling.

For these folks, they want to be able to stay home in their retirement. They want their kids to visit, and they want their grandchildren to visit.

Something that I have noticed with my grandparents, although I was younger and a little less mature, was that travel wasn't as important to them as was spending time with their loved ones. I am beginning to see the same desire with my parents now. It's a treat to be able to spend time with their children and their extended families.

While my parents still like to travel, go to music concerts, and see things all around the world, they really enjoy when everybody gets together for Thanksgiving and any other holiday.

That may be your dream — to travel to see loved ones — and, if your loved ones live in the same country, typically the cost to travel is less than if you were traveling out of country. However, traveling within the country is still something that needs to be considered in your plan if this is your idea of perfect retirement.

## Continuing to Work

My mom retired early because she evaluated the benefits from her employer, and the employer was seeking to make changes to those benefits. It made more sense for her to retire a little earlier than originally planned. However, her retirement didn't last long. Her former boss and work associate called and asked her to go back to work and help on a part-time basis, but that is not in my mom's nature. When my mom does something, she does it all out. That was probably six or seven years ago, and she is still working today.

Retirement and no longer having a place to go every day is not for everybody. I've met plenty of seventy- and eighty-year-old folks who are financially able to stop working altogether, but that is not how they are wired. It wouldn't make them happy. Retirement is not something that they want—they prefer to continue working.

The first day of my dad's retirement was spent walking around the house. I asked mom how he was doing and she said, "He's just kind of wandering around, trying to figure out what to do. As long as he stays out of my way, we'll be fine."

As mentioned, retirement is not for everybody. Continuing to work doesn't mean you continue with your regular job. An option that many retirees take is getting involved in volunteer work—a nonprofit whose work they value or their church.

Many retirees want to feel like they are contributing to society, they have so much more to give, and they have valuable skills that are in demand in the nonprofit sector. Sixty-five or seventy doesn't have to be the end of a fulfilling and engaging life for retirees, and many people—and society as a whole—are better off because of it.

Many of the clients I have worked with continue to do some type of work and fill a valuable role in society.

# CHAPTER *FIVE*

# Planning Your Legacy

## THE DANGER IN NOT PLANNING

When we don't plan, we put ourselves at risk of not being as efficient as we can be. This could mean that we don't have as much money to leave as a legacy. It could also mean that more money goes to the government than we wanted.

The purpose of planning is to make sure that we are being as efficient in as many areas as possible. We want to maximize the money that we have for our lifetime, and we want to maximize the amount of money that we leave to our children and grandchildren.

Therefore, retirement planning is not just looking at one individual piece. It is looking at all these different parts and at the picture as a whole because they all work together to ensure efficiencies for you and to minimize what is going to the government. Planning maximizes your chances of achieving what you want.

My grandfather taught me *The Six P Principle* a long time ago, and my father repeated it. I have heard that it originated in the military as marines have mentioned it to me in the past. This applies to everything.

*The Six P Principle: Proper planning prevents piss-poor performance.*

Another great saying that I've come to love is: *Failing to plan is just like planning to fail.*

The three important areas where planning is critical for your success down the road are:

- Taxes
- Investments
- Legal documents

But, it's also about health and insurance. We should sit down and tie all these components together during the planning process. Looking at all the pieces together is what determines the long-term success of your plan.

Unfortunately, that's something that is completely missing in today's financial world. People working in this field simply focus on one thing, and it's usually the sale of the product. What I'm sharing is a different discussion that fills a different need. It is something that everybody should have.

## You Pay Too Much in Taxes

Of course, death and taxes are the two inevitable things in life. One of the first things you get is a social security number so that the government can track your income and your taxes. It's not any different in retirement. When you don't plan properly, you could find yourself in a position where you are paying more in taxes than you should.

Tax planning, as we discussed earlier, is about the art of looking forward. It's the art of creating systems and plans that will minimize your taxes throughout the rest of your life. In retirement, that is incredibly important.

You need to look at your expenses and think of ways to lower them as much as possible. You want to minimize the taxes that you pay on your social security; if it's below a certain amount, you don't have to pay tax on social security, or, at the very least, the amount you pay is minimized.

Too many people have only taxable accounts, 401(k)s, 403(b)s, IRAs, which means that when you withdraw money from these accounts, you pay tax on them.

What if you converted some of those to Roth accounts?

What if you had money invested in after-tax accounts, which would mean that when you sold them or took money out, you only had to pay capital gains tax instead of ordinary income tax?

That could result in a huge tax savings.

Planning is so incredibly important when it comes to the amount in taxes we wind up paying over our lifetimes. Of course, we should pay what we owe, but we can also put strategies in place to minimize that amount over our life and even over our children's lives as we pass money down to our family.

## Your Assets Go to the Government

This concept speaks to both taxes and estate planning. When you don't do proper retirement planning, you could end up paying more in taxes than if you had planned earlier in life, or if you had looked at your financial situation from a long-term perspective. Paying more in taxes is one way that your assets go to the government rather than staying within your family.

Another way assets are lost to the government is by not doing proper estate planning. If you don't have your legal documents written properly or if you don't have your retirement or your bank accounts titled properly, they could go through the probate system. There could be fees and costs and additional taxes applied.

Money over a certain amount is subject to federal estate taxes or even estate state taxes. Those taxes don't apply in Florida, but there are a lot of places that do have estate state taxes. With proper planning, you would be alerted to this and strategize to minimize that by, for example, gifting. If you don't plan for this, you're just going to be giving more money to the government.

That's obviously something that you want to look at from all different angles. You want to look at this from the estate planning side, the tax planning side, and the investment side. The type of investments you have determines that type of taxes you pay.

Taking all these combined components into consideration when planning will minimize the amount of money that goes to the government.

**You Make Poor Investment Choices**

In reviewing the portfolios of clients on a regular basis, one thing I have noticed is that people continue to be stuck in the mode of continual growth. For years, we have been in this accumulation phase of our lives when we know that we must save and invest for our money to grow. At a certain point, we need to start to rely on that money to provide us with an income, and stable growth. In other words, we need to start living off that money.

The same investment strategy that you used when you were forty and fifty years old is probably not going to be the right investment strategy as you get older—into your sixties and beyond. There are all sorts of rules of thumb around how much you should have in aggressive investments versus conservative ones. However, it's not that simple—those are just rules of thumb.

Your amount of risk and the way your portfolio is put together need to be tied to your goals and your personal financial situation. Having investments that you had ten, fifteen, twenty years ago is not appropriate at every age. They need to evolve and change—but not based on some simple algorithm that merely says you are getting older. It needs to be based on your life, your needs, and your goals.

Avoiding making bad investments choices can save you thousands, even hundreds of thousands of dollars, depending on how much money you have. Someone who has invested way too aggressively in 2008, would be hurt a lot more than someone that invested conservatively in the same year when the stock market came tumbling down.

As you retire, that last thing that you need is to be counting on an investment growing or staying where it is. Investing too aggressively is risky, and your investments have the potential of not being available to you when you need them the most. Making poor investment choices is one reason you need to be aware. You may need a second opinion to make sure that your portfolio is put together appropriately for your specific situation.

**Emergencies**

No one wants to be a burden on our children, but emergencies are going to come up in our lives. Emergencies inevitably occur and having money set aside because you have planned for these potential events means that they don't throw you off balance when they do occur.

A healthcare emergency is typically one of the most crucial, so it's important to be able to act swiftly. Having money set aside for medical emergencies allows you to do that.

Here in Florida, we are susceptible to hurricanes. If your property sustains damage during a hurricane, your emergency fund will be used. Maybe you have an old tree in your yard and it falls on your garage in high winds. Your emergency fund will take care of that.

Because your emergency fund needs to be accessed quickly, and at any time, it's not going to be invested in a product that will provide you with a great return. It's meant to be money that you can count on in case you need it.

When you plan for emergencies and set money aside for this purpose, you don't have to rely on retirement accounts, savings, credit cards, or borrowing money to address any emergency that may come up.

## FAMILY

For me, family is incredibly important. I am close to my family. I feel that I always have been and even though we don't all live together, we still talk with one another and keep in touch. I have also seen that in how my parents grew up and their relationships with their parents.

One of the most innate things in humans is to give our offspring something better than what we had ourselves. For so many of my clients, that is their focus or goal. Sometimes it's a husband who wants to make sure that his wife is going to be taken care of. Or it's a mother who wants to help her children.

We absolutely want to do the best that we can for our family. That's why proper planning is of critical importance to make sure we can do what we want to help our family, to leave as much as we possibly can for our loved ones.

I want to repeat that giving to family is not just about leaving money—it's about your life. It's about taking care of the people you love. For some, that will take the form of money. For others, it's about preserving the relationships, spending quality time together, and maybe even going on vacation together.

Giving to family could also mean the ability to spend holidays together, or to gather at a special location to enjoy a sunny summer afternoon visiting, talking, or playing cards. There are a few card players in my family. We often get together to play cards, and we find it's a great way to visit.

It's important to plan to make sure you can live the life you envision for yourself and your family. While it may not be common to have this type of conversation when you are looking at your stock portfolio, it's an important aspect to include in your financial plan to make sure it provides for you.

### Children and Grandchildren

Helping kids is one of the things that so many people want to do, whether it's from a financial perspective or an education perspective. My grandparents, in addition to doing a wonderful job raising their families, also wanted to provide for their grandchildren.

In addition to helping my mom and dad through college, they also set aside money for my brothers, my sister, my cousins, and myself to pay for our college educations. It's a huge gift to provide an education for your children and your grandchildren so that they can start their careers without massive debt.

Education is important in my family, and my grandparents made it possible for all of us to go out into the world and begin our careers with a solid education.

Many clients I've worked with want to leave a legacy — money for their children and grandchildren. This could be in the form of money so that family members are secure, or they want to grow a business and pass it on, ensuring the family name lives on forever.

On the flip side of this, many clients — and this is common among baby boomers — don't want to be a burden to their children as they get older. They want to live their lives independently, and they want to do things independently. They want their children and grandchildren to be with them and remember them in happy times — not to be a burden to them in any way, financially, physically, or otherwise.

Providing for children and grandchildren is a big deal for so many people. As a child who looks up to their parents and grandparents, you remember the things they did for you, especially as you get older. You think about the things they sacrificed, the time and care they took to prepare lunches, or driving to numerous baseball or soccer practices and games.

As we get older, we want to do that for our kids and for our grandkids because we know what it feels like now. I think that is really the heart and soul of why this is such an important part of planning from a financial perspective: to make sure we can afford to do what we want and to provide for our children and grandchildren.

## Parents

As parents get older, many people want to repay them. After all, they cared for you and provided for you. They may have reached a point where they need your help. You may want to be there for them in some way, including moving them into your own home.

My great grandmother lived in our home, and my grandparents spent a lot of time helping care for her as she got older. As my grandmother got older, my mom, uncle, and aunt all took turns having her live in their homes. It was their preferred alternative to having her go to a nursing home.

Some elderly persons have issues that require nursing home care, but for healthy individuals, staying in their own home is preferable. They want their kids and grandkids to visit and assist when needed in the comfort of their own home. That is what we did for both sides of my family, both sets of grandparents, we allowed them to age in place, and we were available to help take care of them.

I think that's the way that most people want to do things. Even though baby boomers don't want to be a burden, there are still a lot of people that want to help take care of their parents. As people get older, this way of helping aging parents is going to be more and more popular.

In fact, it may be something that needs to happen as the cost of nursing homes and skilled nursing care skyrockets. As the population ages, those costs continue to increase. For many people, this option is simply not affordable.

As part of your analysis and planning, you need to look at these costs.

Can you afford to go into a nursing home?

You can get a long-term policy that covers it. All these things must be taken into consideration and discussed during the planning process.

## PHILANTHROPY

More and more people want to give back to the places and organizations that have meant so much to them in their lives. For example, many people want to give back to their educational organizations, their churches, or their local hospital. It's human nature to want to give, and I believe we get more from giving than we do from receiving.

During retirement, many of our clients volunteer, which is another way of giving back, or they leave a legacy to their favorite organizations. In your planning process, identify where you want to give back so you can achieve that goal.

Giving money to people and places that we love and that have helped us along the way is something that is so important to so many people. Often, people don't think about how they give, and they don't take time to plan their gifts.

There are legal structures that you can set up to give away appreciated stock or real estate, for example, and you need to ascertain the fees associated with that. Many financial advisors don't ask their clients whether they want to give back.

Consider the following:

- Does your financial advisor ask you about the charities you want to give to?

- Does he or she ask you what kind of legacy you want to leave behind for your children and your grandchildren?

- Do you want to give to a foundation, a hospital, or a hospice type of organization?

- Do you want to establish a scholarship with a university?

Please be sure to discuss your wishes for philanthropy with your financial advisor because you want to make sure you are setting this up the proper way. It's a huge opportunity and think how great you will feel.

**Church**

Most people are spiritual in some way, shape, or form—or they practice some type of faith. For many, their spiritual life becomes stronger as life goes on.

We have our beliefs here in our company, and they guide the way that we do our planning. It guides the way that we make decisions for people, and it guides the way that we run this company. We are going to do what is in everybody's best interest, and the church is a huge part of what influences us.

When people retire, they often want to give back to their church, perhaps by participating more often, as it helps them feel a stronger spiritual connection. Leaving money to your church provides many advantages in retirement that many people aren't aware of.

If you want to give money to your church, there are tax advantages to doing that. If you wish to leave money to family and to your church, identifying assets — such as an IRA to go to your church instead of a life insurance policy or a brokerage account — can have major tax ramifications. Churches that qualify as charities are not required to pay taxes on donated individual retirement accounts.

However, your children and grandchildren would be subject to paying taxes on an IRA. Proper planning helps maximize the amount of money that is available to allocate.

## Causes or Charities

We have a lot of clients who participate in various charitable organizations, and we try to support as many of them as we possibly can every year. That is something we do as a company because we believe in giving back to our local community, in addition to what we contribute personally. Many of our clients give back in the form of supporting a local cause or charity.

For example, the local community hospice had done a wonderful job making my paternal grandmother comfortable, so after she passed away we assembled many items to donate back to them as a way of contributing to our local community.

Giving back to local causes that are close to you is something that can take many forms. If you wish to give money to causes or charities, planning to do it right can have a positive financial impact for, not only the charity, but also you and your family.

## Scholarship Funds

This is something I've thought about a lot. When I was studying to become a certified financial planner, one of my teachers said to me, "You know Mike, when you finish all these courses, you take the two-day test, and you have the experience, requirements, and everything else to become a certified financial planner, you are still going to be minimally qualified to call yourself a financial planner."

I recall laughing and thought to myself: *what have I been doing for the last couple of years?*

But I've come to realize that he was right.

The certified financial planner education is the base, the foundation that you build on. Your life experience continues the education from there. It's the same whether you study to become an engineer, a pilot, a social worker, or a history teacher. You are taught the basics that you are going to use for the rest of your life, and that becomes something that is cherished.

It's cherished over our lifetime because this education is what allows us to go out and work, earn an income, be a part of society, and set money aside so that one day we can retire.

Giving back doesn't end with providing for our family and donating to our local church. Often, people want to give back to the institutions that made them who they are, that had such a huge influence on their lives, and gave them the foundation for their chosen profession.

Funding scholarships is a great way to give back, as is donating to help construct a new building or refurbish an existing one. Setting aside money for education is always a worthy cause. A lot of people do this, and I salute them for it.

# *Conclusion*

I hope this book has opened your eyes. I hope you realize that the financial services industry, Wall Street, and everyone working with investment money has done a huge disservice to people across this country. I truly feel that the focus is too much on money instead of your life as a whole. Ultimately, your life is the most important thing there is.

Everything that we do, everything that we have saved for, everything that we have done up to this point is so that we can live our lives the way that we want to—the life of our dreams. It's about having a life of relaxation and enjoyment, of happiness and tears, and time with family and friends if that is what we choose for ourselves.

But unfortunately, the rest of the financial industry focuses on selling you something or profiting from your savings. I personally don't think that is right. I think it's shortsighted and possibly the worst thing for you. I think it is not the right way to treat people.

I view this type of business as something incredibly noble when done in service of others. That's the way I approach financial planning, and that has been my mission from the beginning. This is much more than investments or a career for me; it's my way of helping people.

There are many areas where people need help. Again, I think people deserve better than what they are getting. I think people need to be guided to look at the bigger picture. I think that they need to work with a team. Yes, the investments are part of it, but there is so much more.

Ultimately, we should figure out a way and do everything we can to make sure that we are achieving what you want, achieving your goals, whatever they may be. I want people to seriously consider what they have done up to this point. We want to look at your investments, your portfolio, and your life as a whole.

Do you just have a bucket of investments?

Do you have a plan?

If you don't have a plan that has been analyzed, if you are not working with somebody who has talked to you about your goals, your spending habits, your health and analyzed your current assets and holdings, then your investments may not be working at optimum for you.

Have you established how you are you going to pass your assets on to your family?

What are your healthcare costs?

Unless you are working with somebody who has taken everything into consideration, your financial plan may be lacking, and you may be wondering if you will have enough money to do the things you want to do. You may also be wondering whether you will outlive the savings that you have.

Maybe these thoughts going through your head:

*I hope that we don't get sick and need to spend a whole bunch of money on long-term care for my spouse or myself.*

*I hope that my children don't have to take care of me.*

Hope is not a plan. Hope is when you don't want to put the time into making sure that you have a plan.

My goal is guiding people to consider where they are now, what they have, and establishing a plan that guarantees them success in getting where they want to go in the future. I want them to feel safe in the knowledge that they can handle the pitfalls that are going to come their way. Lastly, I want them to know that they can enjoy the retirement they have dreamed about, and that they can pass on their assets to their families.

The plan that looks at all these things is what determines how you should be invested. You should not have investments that you can't explain or understand. You shouldn't have investments that you worry about. You should know that what you have done is going to be enough to accomplish everything that you want.

I want people to seriously look at those things and if you just have investments, and you don't have that plan, I want you to reach out to somebody who can help put that plan together. This country is filled with certified financial planners — good planners across the country — who can help you do this.

A good planner looks at you as a person, not just as number or a statistic, and puts together a financial plan that it is going to consider all these things.

Don't be afraid to ask them questions:

- Are you a fiduciary?
- Are you going to look at my goals?
- Are you going to provide me with an investment strategy, or is this a long-term relationship?

Additionally, I want people to act. The number of people in this country who have not done any type of planning is staggering. It doesn't matter how old you are, how young you are, how much or how little you have saved, where you come from or where you are going. You need to have a written financial plan, and you need to review it and update it, constantly.

If you don't have one simply because you haven't taken the time to do so, make the call. Find somebody now. If you have a plan, but you have not kept up with it, that's another problem. You must update and monitor your plan. Everything is going to change — taxes, investments, the legal side of things, and healthcare costs are all going to change.

It doesn't matter who is sitting in the White House, who controls Congress, or who does anything. All that is constantly going to change. Putting a plan together once and then forgetting about it isn't enough because, as much as all those other things change, the biggest changes are within us. We change.

Our life changes; our goals may change. We may get thrown for a loop; we may inherit or win money. We should make sure that all those changes are taken into consideration by updating and monitoring our plans. So, if you haven't done that recently, you need to do that as well.

This business does not take care of people. Too often, I find, people will sell an investment and take their money and run. There is no incentive for them to follow up with you. That must change.

There is more to this business. There is more to retirement planning than just looking at some parts of the picture, generating commissions, and running away. It's about your lifestyle. It's about your life.

First and foremost, this is lifestyle planning, and you should work with people who are in it to help you.

# Next Steps

Michael specializes in holistic, integrated financial planning, focusing on you as an individual and your family. Putting your needs ahead of his own is part of his duty as a fiduciary. He is a public speaker and educator who also works with families to create retirement plans that focus on their goals.

To speak with Michael directly, you may contact him at: Michael@petrosplanning.com or 904-824-5656.

# About the Author

Michael K. Macke, CFP

President, Petros Advisory Services, LLC, Principal Advisor

Michael Macke is President of Petros Advisory Services and Vice-President and co-owner of Petros Estate & Retirement Planning, a company headquartered in Jacksonville, Florida with offices in St. Augustine and Winter Park. He is also vice-president and co-owner of Woman's Worth®, a financial planning firm focused on the unique planning needs of women. He believes in education, transparency, honesty, and integrity, qualities he learned from his grandparents and parents.

Michael feels Petros and Woman's Worth® are here to serve others, and there is great nobility in that cause.

He takes a great deal of time in getting to know every person he sits down with so their retirement plan is customized to them and designed to achieve their unique goals.

He joined the firm in the summer of 2013, after over thirteen years as an advisor with a large retirement investment group. He has over twenty years' experience in banking and financial services and has been a Certified Financial Planner® professional for more than ten years.

Michael focuses on personal financial planning and wealth preservation for those close to and already in retirement, their families, and legacy planning for their heirs. He brings a passion for helping people identify, achieve, and protect their retirement lifestyle dreams.

As a CFP® professional, Michael has completed extensive training and experience requirements and is held to rigorous ethical standards. He understands the complexities of the changing financial climate and will always make recommendations that are in his client's best interests.

Michael has lived in Jacksonville for most of his life, having moved to the area in 1980. He has worked with various local organizations professionally and personally, including Community Hospice of NE Florida, UF Health, Goodwill Industries of NE Florida, and he is an active member of the Notre Dame Club of Jacksonville.

When he is not working, Michael enjoys spending time with family and friends, playing golf, and relaxing at the beach.

www.ingramcontent.com/pod-product-compliance
Lightning Source LLC
Chambersburg PA
CBHW052122090426
42741CB00009B/1919